FAITH IS THE VICTORY

Ron & Ryan Sutton

Unless otherwise indicated, all Scripture quotations are taken from the New International Version (NIV) of the Bible.

Copyright © 2023 Ron & Ryan Sutton

All rights reserved.

ISBN: 9798375958194

To order materials or schedule meetings

P.O. Box 21, Crystal City, Missouri 63019

314-960-8308

www.RyanSutton.org

www.TheGraceCenter.com

CONTENTS

	INTRODUCTION	1
1	FAITH IS THE VICTORY	15
2	FAITH IN THE UNSEEN	41
3	FAITH TO COME OUT OF THE CAVE	53
4	FAITH THAT DOESN'T FAINT	65
5	DESPERATE FAITH	79
6	FAITH TO SLAY A GIANT	111
7	FAITH IN THE BLOOD	141
	WHY AM I HERE? WHAT IS MY PURPOSE?	167

INTRODUCTION

REAL FAITH

Faith is more than believing; it is more than believing and confessing. Talk is cheap. The devils believe but they don't have faith (James 2:19). Faith is believing and obeying. True Bible faith is always expressed with actions, not just words. True Bible faith is expressed and revealed by obedience. A great example of faith expressing itself in obedience is found in Hebrews 11:8: "By faith Abraham, when called to go to a place he would later receive as his inheritance, obeyed and went, even though he did not know where he was going."

Real faith is a product of the spiritual realm, not the material. Paul says faith is a fruit of the Spirit (Galatians 5:22, KJV) and also a gift of the Spirit (1 Corinthians 12:9). The proof of genuine faith is not material prosperity. Some of the greatest men and women of faith throughout Church history did not experience material prosperity, but they did great exploits through faith. The Apostle Paul endured long periods of struggle and hardship and he had strong faith. In fact, he received his revelation of faith personally from Jesus when he was taken up to the third heaven (2 Corinthians 12:21). He never pointed to material prosperity as evidence of his faith, but no one would question that he possessed great faith.

Paul had genuine faith that rose up in victory no matter how trying the circumstances. When he was on the way to a prayer meeting in Philippi he cast a demon out of a young slave girl – a spirit of divination which enabled her to predict the future. Her owners were infuriated because she made them a lot of money and after the demon was cast out, she was unable to practice divination. They stirred up a mob and Paul and Silas were severely beaten and thrown into prison. Such trials would shake my faith –

most people's faith – but not the Apostle Paul's. The Bible tells us that at midnight Paul and Silas began to sing praises to God (Acts 16:16-40). God answered with an earthquake, their chains fell off, and the jailer and his family were saved. That is the victory of genuine faith. Paul's life was not marked by unending material prosperity but testimonies of overcoming faith rising with victory out of suffering.

Paul was popular in Lystra, a city in Turkey, after a crippled man was healed. But his enemies soon turned popular opinion against him, and he was stoned by an angry mob and left for dead. That didn't stop him! While some of the believers were gathered around him, he got up and went back into the city (Acts 14:8-20). He attacked the kingdom of darkness wherever he went, and the forces of darkness did everything possible to stop him. He experienced these attacks because of faith, not because of a lack of it.

His faith was never shaken by lack, hardship, or suffering. Here is his testimony in Philippians 4: 11-14: "I am not saying this because I am in need, for I have learned to be content whatever the circumstances. I know what it is to be in need, and I know what it is to have plenty. I have learned the secret of being content in any and every situation, whether well fed or hungry, whether living in plenty or in want. I can do all this through him who gives me strength."

As his life on earth drew to a close, Paul suffered as a prisoner in Rome. He knows that martyrdom awaits him, but he is still speaking faith. There is no whining, complaining or self-pity. We find him writing an epistle to Timothy as he awaits death. Some of his final words on earth stand as an immortal testimony of real faith that rises with victory out of suffering. "For I am already being poured out like a drink offering, and the time for my departure is near. I have fought the good fight, I have finished the race, I have kept the faith. Now there is in store for me the crown of righteousness, which the

Lord, the righteous Judge, will award to me on that day and not only to me, but also to all who have longed for his appearing" (2 Timothy 4:6-8).

This book is not just a rehash of the same message of faith you have heard over and over again. It is not words borrowed from modern faith preachers and repackaged with a slightly different slant. Our purpose in this writing is to present the victorious message of authentic Bible faith. If you read just a few pages, we believe you will see that this is different. The message of faith presented here is rooted in the Bible, not metaphysical theology, or positive mind science.

Authentic Bible faith will work anywhere in the world, not just in prosperous, materialistic nations. The following pages contain a straightforward presentation of victorious faith lived out in the Bible. There will be none of the fundraising schemes or gimmicks employed by many of the purveyors of the modern faith message. You will find none of the cunning attempts to get you to sow a seed for your need which are so common on Christian television, in newsletters and in meetings today. The message set forth here is not designed to enrich the preacher; it is freely given, as it was freely received, with the sincere hope that it will help people who are struggling

- especially those who have been disillusioned or discouraged by a modern faith message which has often been found sadly lacking in love. Authentic Bible faith has always been "faith that works by love" (Galatians 5:6).

It is our prayer that the message of faith presented in the following chapters will help you rise up and enter into a greater dimension of victory. If you are one of the many who has been frustrated by some selfish perversion of authentic Bible faith, we pray that you will see the difference between the counterfeit and the genuine and find the strength to run again. God is a giver, not a taker. Men have used faith to manipulate and take from you. God wants to right that wrong; He wants to give you a fresh revelation of faith that will lift you up and send you forward with new hope in your heart. He has no games or gimmicks. He sincerely loves you and wants to give you faith that will help in your time of need. God loves you and wants the best for you. He has no selfish motives. He wants you to be blessed by growing in and exercising authentic Bible faith.

It is our prayer that this book will help you on your journey. God has more for us. The faith we see modeled in the Bible did not always escape trials and suffering, but it always came through them with an attitude of victory. If you, like so many sincere believers today, are passing through hard times, you are in good company. Listen to David in Psalm 27:13-14, "I would have lost heart, unless I had believed that I would see the goodness of the LORD in the land of the living. Wait on the LORD; Be of good courage, And He shall strengthen your heart; Wait, I say, on the LORD" (NKJV)!

The Apostle Peter had victorious faith. Do you remember what Jesus said to Peter in Luke 22: 31-32? "Simon, Simon, Satan has asked to sift all of you as wheat. But I have prayed for you, Simon, that your faith may not fail. And when you have turned back, strengthen your brothers."

We know that Simon Peter failed Jesus after this discussion. He fell hard. He actually denied that he was a follower of Jesus, or that he even knew Him. There are those who say that Jesus' prayer was not answered because Peter failed. But we must look at the prayer more carefully. Jesus didn't pray that Peter would not fail; He prayed that his faith would not fail. Take note: Peter failed but his faith didn't. Perhaps you have had the same experience. You failed Jesus and now the devil is condemning you. It is time to get up and go on with Jesus just like Peter did. Jesus didn't leave Peter in his failure and condemnation. He loved him and went searching for him. Peter's faith took hold of love and forgiveness and got back in the race. Faith took him up the stairs to the Upper Room where he was baptized in the power of the Spirit on the Day of Pentecost. Bible faith can transform fearful disciples into courageous preachers. What it did for Peter it can do for you.

This book does not make material prosperity the status symbol of faith. This is a book about faith that overcomes; it is about the kind of faith that will pick you up out of the dirt, dust you off, and send you on your way with renewed hope of victory. This is a book about authentic Bible faith – the kind that looks the devil in the eye and boldly proclaims,

"Forward ever, backward never! I'm coming through in Jesus' name!"

1

FAITH IS THE VICTORY

Faith in Jesus is the key to victory in life. Jesus faced everything that defeats us in this world and prevailed. He triumphed over Satan and all the powers of darkness as a man. He overcame them by the power of the Holy Spirit and by the Word of God, and we can overcome them in the same way. Jesus is committed to help you cross the finish line of life with victory in your soul. He is able to keep you by His mighty power: "… in all these things we are more than conquerors through him who loved us. For I am convinced that neither death nor life, neither angels nor demons, neither the present nor the future, nor any powers, neither height nor depth, nor anything else in all creation, will be able to separate us from the love of God that is in Christ Jesus our Lord" (Romans 8:37-39). "… for I know whom I have believed and am persuaded that He is able to keep what I have committed to Him until that Day" (2 Timothy 1:12, NKJV).

Paul's faith didn't help him avoid or escape trial and tribulation, but it brought him through with the confidence of a conqueror.

What kind of a man could pass through the list of hardships Paul outlined in Romans 8 and then proclaim that in all these things we are more than conquerors? Only a man with authentic Bible faith could stand up under such intense onslaughts from hell and refuse to wave the white flag of surrender. Not only did he refuse to surrender; he proclaimed victory in the face of what looked like certain failure. He kept fighting when all his strength was gone. He kept trusting in the power of God when he was overcome with human weakness.

We have talked with pastors who said Paul suffered because of a failure in his faith, or because he let down in his confession. We say that Paul suffered because he had great faith – faith that made the devil madder than you and I ever have. Paul's faith got him in a lot of trouble, but the same faith that got him in trouble brought him back out with victory time and time again. The devil doesn't know what to do with believers like Paul. He did things to him that would have made most grown men cry "Mama," but Paul wouldn't even say ouch.

In the introduction, we mentioned Paul's experience at Philippi. He knew he was in the will of God; a vision directed him there. But that didn't keep him from being beaten and thrown into prison. At midnight singing was heard from the depths of the dungeon. Paul and Silas weren't feeling sorry for themselves or crying; they were praising God. Heaven got so excited over such a sacrifice of praise that things really got stirred up. The events that took place that night mess with the natural mind. Praise went up and power came down. The praise was answered with an earthquake, doors started opening and chains fell off the prisoners. The greatest miracle of the night was that not one of the prisoners ran. The jailor and his whole household were saved and baptized.

If you were the devil, what would you do with a man like the Apostle Paul? How would you stop him? Hardship and persecution served only to refine his faith and strengthen his resolve. He didn't care about driving the finest car, wearing the nicest clothes, flying first class, or staying in the best hotel in town. He was happy to be in a prison cell if he was there in the will of God. He was content whether in poverty or in prosperity; he knew how to be abased and how to abound. He shouted victory and rose up in faith regardless of the circumstances. His faith enabled him to say in all honesty, "…for I have learned to be content whatever the circumstances" (Philippians 4:11).

Paul's faith could function as effectively in a poor nation as in a prosperous one. He was more interested in using faith to fight the devil than to pursue prosperity. He had faith that was more focused on doing something than on getting something. His lifestyle might not impress or appeal to prosperity preachers, but it sure got the devil's attention. The devils lost sleep whenever Paul was in town.

As we saw in the preceding pages, Paul wouldn't even back up for the devil when he had been beaten to the point of death. Legalistic religious leaders stirred up a mob to stone him outside of Lystra. They left him lying in a pool of blood, certain he was dead. But when they got back to town Paul was there – alive and well. He probably picked up his sermon where he left off when they drug him out of town (Acts 14:19-20). Can you find that kind of faith anywhere today? Sure, you can — even in America. But if you want to see a lot of it, you will have to go to nations like China where believers don't run from sacrifice or suffering. The believers there care more about winning souls than about making merchandise of the people of God. They don't preach a gospel of gain, but they are gaining ground every day. The Church in China is stronger than in America. Faith has laid down in the lap of prosperity in America. In China, authentic Bible faith has endured persecution, passed through the flood and the fire, and refused to back up for anything. It has risen up victorious out of suffering to lead the Church from victory to victory and glory to glory.

We smuggled Bibles into China in the 1980's and 1990's. We knew the devil was in trouble the first time we looked into the eyes of persecuted believers in the underground Church. We saw pain and trauma in the eyes of those persecuted saints that humbled us deeply. But we also saw the light of overcoming faith that said, "I love not my life unto the death" (Revelation 12:11). The gates of hell have not prevailed against the Church in China. Hell burned their Bibles, tortured, imprisoned, and killed their leaders. The powers of darkness tormented the true believers in every manner possible. The devil took out all the stops and tried to obliterate the Church in China; he failed. The devil is sick and dying in China; Jesus is alive and well. The prosperity seeking, comfort loving faith often found in America is a fragile thing next to the faith of persecuted believers in China. Their plight should inspire us, not frighten us. They are living proof that the One who lives in us is greater than the ruler of the darkness of this world. They have proved beyond reasonable doubt that faith – real faith – is the victory that overcomes the world.

You need not fear the coming storm. Jesus has promised to never leave or forsake you. You will never have to fight a battle alone.

You can count on Him to always do what is promised in Isaiah 41:10: "So do not fear, for I am with you; do not be dismayed, for I am your God. I will strengthen you and help you. I will uphold you with my righteous right hand." Life may be hard for you right now. You may be in the worst battle of your life. Don't give up. Don't give in to discouragement. Jesus is with you. You can't lose if you hold on to Him. Faith will bring you through to the victory side.

The faith practiced by a large segment of the modern Church often leaves people frustrated. It is there for them when things are going well, but they often feel deserted in the hard times. True Bible faith never fails. It is with you through it all – in good times and hard times. It will pick you up when you fall down and encourage you to keep going. It will strengthen you when you feel like you are too weak to take another step. The problem with the faith of the modern Church often comes because it places too much emphasis on using faith to get something from God, instead of exercising faith to live a victorious life. The emphasis of faith in the New Testament Church emphasized doing something for God, or with God, as much as it emphasized obtaining something from God.

It was an active faith that focused more on pleasing God than on satisfying self. It was focused more on the spiritual than on the material. Bible faith treated the world more as a battleground than a playground. It produced a victorious Church that took the fight to the enemy – a Church that attacked the gates of hell and prevailed. It was a faith that lived with a great commitment to the Great Commission. It placed more emphasis on extending the Kingdom of God than on increasing material substance. It faced danger and hardship with a victorious attitude and relentlessly challenged the darkness. New Testament faith was more interested in making the devil uncomfortable than in surrounding itself with material comfort. It transformed cringing cowards into fearless preachers. It caused men to repent and demons to tremble. It chose confrontation over compromise and refused to make peace with the world, the flesh, or the devil.

Authentic Bible faith concerned itself more with confronting and changing the culture than it did with becoming relevant or culture current. It was a kingdom conscious faith that declared war on the world system rather than trying to make peace with it. It never viewed the world as a misunderstood friend but as a mortal enemy. It was a faith that worked by love (Galatians 5:6) but it had no love for the world. It was after people. It waged perpetual warfare against the spirit of the world with authority from Jesus to preach a Gospel of power. Bible faith refused to retreat even in the face of severe opposition and persecution. It met every enemy along the road with the full force of heaven and marched steadily onward and upward. It carried the Gospel to the entire known world in less than a century without television, printing presses, the internet, or social media. Bible faith got the job done by relying on the Holy Spirit and preaching the Word of God with force and conviction.

The evil of this present age will eat us alive unless we part ways with the soft, selfish faith of the moment and return to the fighting faith of the New Testament. Authentic Bible faith is engaged in mortal combat - a fight to the death - with three enemies: the world, the flesh, and the devil:

"Do not love the world or anything in the world. If anyone loves the world, love for the Father is not in them. For everything in the world—the lust of the flesh, the lust of the eyes, and the pride of life—comes not from the Father but from the world. The world and its desires pass away, but whoever does the will of God lives forever (1 John 2:15-17).

The good news is that the sincere believer who possesses authentic Bible faith is destined to overcome every enemy:

The world - "For everyone born of God overcomes the world. This is the victory that has overcome the world, even our faith. Who is it that overcomes the world? Only the one who believes that Jesus is the Son of God" (1 John 5:4-5).

The flesh – "What a wretched man I am! Who will rescue me from this body that is subject to death? Thanks be to God, who delivers me through Jesus Christ our Lord" (Romans 7:24-25).

The devil – "You, dear children, are from God and have overcome them, because the one who is in you is greater than the one who is in the world" (I John 4:4).

Negative circumstances do not negate the victory of faith. We are victorious by faith whether or not we feel victorious. It is an established fact. Our victory comes through faith in the finished work of Jesus on the Cross. We are victorious when things are going well and when everything seems to be falling apart. Our victory is not rooted in feelings or circumstances. Our victory is certain because it depends by faith on nothing less than Jesus' blood and righteousness. When we fear that we are losing our hold on victory we can still rejoice; at those moments victory is holding on to us. Faith is the victory. Maybe your faith has shrunk to the size of a mustard seed. Don't panic: That is enough. The power that has come to us is greater than we know. One drop of holy blood appropriated by faith is enough to wash away all our sin. Faith the size of a mustard seed is enough to do the devil in:

"Then I heard a loud voice in heaven say: "Now have come the salvation and the power and the kingdom of our God, and the authority of his Christ. For the accuser of our brothers, who accuses them before our God day and night, has been hurled down. They overcame him by the blood of the Lamb and by the word of their testimony; they did not love their lives so much as to shrink from death" (Revelation 12:10-11).

FAITH IS THE VICTORY

When faith appropriates the power of the blood of Jesus, victory is certain. Victorious faith has a testimony. By that testimony Satan is overcome. It is a testimony about Jesus and the power of the blood He shed for us. Are demons attacking you with thoughts of failure and defeat? Don't have a sinking spell. This is your opportunity to exercise faith and proclaim the blood bought victory of Calvary. Demons will hate you for doing that. Don't panic. If a multitude comes against you, hold your ground. Faith is the victory. Jesus in you is greater than all the hosts of darkness arrayed against you. Are they bombarding your mind with negative thoughts and trying to provoke you to panic?

You don't have to sit passively and listen to them. A great victory has been won: tell them about it – remind them of it.

Invite the whole miserable lot – or legion – of them to pull up a chair and listen to what you have to say. Declare with all boldness, "I have a testimony for you." Testify to demons: Why not? Jesus did it all the time. Consider the fourth chapter of Matthew where Jesus was tempted by the devil. He overcame him the same way you and I must overcome him – by speaking the Word of God. After inviting the demons to pull up a chair and stay awhile, begin testifying. Say, "I have a testimony. It is about the blood. It is about the power of the blood.

Do you want to hear more? Do you know that sin you keep reminding me of? God doesn't even remember it. It is under the blood." Keep talking. I am certain they will begin leaving before the testimony is finished. Faith is the victory!

If there are some stubborn ones, keep testifying. Expand your testimony. Say it out loud. "Devil, you heard my testimony about the blood. Since you are still here, I am going to testify about the anointing that breaks every yoke. Do you remember how you had me bound for all those years? That is all over, devil. A greater One has come to help me. His anointing has broken your yoke off my life."

"How God anointed Jesus of Nazareth with the Holy Spirit and power, and how he went around doing good and healing all who were under the power of the devil, because God was with him" (Acts 10:38). The King James Version says, "healing all who were oppressed of the devil."

You are no longer bound, living under the oppression of the devil. The anointing has broken the yoke of bondage. The truth has set you free. Faith has given you the victory. Now your life has meaning and purpose. You have a mission – a great cause to live for. God has enlisted you in the greatest army that has ever marched on the earth. You have become an ambassador of the Lord Jesus through faith in His name. Now you have the privilege of helping others escape from Satan's bondage and leading them to victory in Jesus. Don't spend another moment listening to the lies of the devil. You are called and chosen by God to help people in need. You are not an insignificant nobody drifting aimlessly through a confusing life in a hostile world. You are a soldier in God's army entrusted with weapons that can set the captives free. Your victory can become their victory. It is your privilege to share it with them.

"You, dear children, are from God and have overcome them, because the one who is in you is greater than the one who is in the world… for everyone born of God overcomes the world. This is the victory that has overcome the world, even our faith. Who is it that overcomes the world? Only the one who believes that Jesus is the Son of God" (1 John 4:4 and 5:4). Faith is the victory.

2

FAITH IN THE UNSEEN

"And Elisha prayed, "Open his eyes, LORD, so that he may see" (2 Kings 6:17)

Elisha was more concerned about what his servant didn't see than about what he did see. His servant saw the Syrian army which had surrounded them. He saw their chariots and horses. He saw their weapons. He realized that the situation was hopeless. Fear caused him to cry out in despair, "Oh no, my lord! What shall we do" (2 Kings 6:15). Elisha was not disturbed at all. He did not entertain fear. His faith-filled response should encourage our hearts. Elisha saw things his servant didn't see. His faith enabled him to believe that even when God's people are outnumbered in the natural realm, we are still the majority. Elisha looked beyond the natural circumstances. He and his servant looked out the same window, but they saw two different things: The servant saw the Syrian army; Elisha saw the army of God. The servant saw with natural eyes; Elisha saw with eyes of faith: "Don't be afraid," the prophet answered. "Those who are with us are more than those who are with them." And Elisha prayed, "Open his eyes, LORD, so that he may see." Then the

LORD opened the servant's eyes, and he looked and saw the hills full of horses and chariots of fire all around Elisha (2 Kings 6:15-17).

Sometimes, what we don't see is more important than what we do see. This truth is so powerfully revealed in 2 Kings 6 that we should consider the story in more detail. The background is found in the conflict between Syria and Israel. Israel seemed to know every move Syria was going to make before they made it. The king of Syria was convinced that there was a spy in his inner circle who was providing intelligence to Israel. In his anger and frustration, he gathered his advisors and demanded that they reveal who it could be:

"Now the king of Syria was making war against Israel; and he consulted with his servants, saying, "My camp will be in such and such a place." And the man of God sent to the king of Israel, saying, "Beware that you do not pass this place, for the Syrians are coming down there." Then the king of Israel sent someone to the place of which the man of God had told him. Thus, he warned him, and he was watchful there, not just once or twice.

"Therefore, the heart of the king of Syria was greatly troubled by this thing; and he called his servants and said to them, "Will you not show me which of us is for the king of Israel?" And one of his servants said, "None, my lord, O king; but Elisha, the prophet who is in Israel, tells the king of Israel the words that you speak in your bedroom." So, he said, "Go and see where he is, that I may send and get him." And it was told him, saying, "Surely he is in Dothan" (2 kings 6:8-13).

That is why Elisha's servant awoke to see the city surrounded by the mighty Syrian army. By faith, Elisha had been seeing and hearing things in the Spirit long before he saw the invisible army of God on the hills with the Syrians. The enraged king was determined to stop this great prophet, but he miscalculated. He had a huge army; Elisha's was bigger, but the King of Syria had no way of knowing that.

He had no faith. He did not possess the capacity to see what Elisha saw. The army of heaven was with Elisha. His faith not only allowed him to see the army; it enabled him to call on God to send some of heaven's army to earth. Help from above is always superior to what we can find here below. Real faith always looks up and waits with expectation for heaven to come and help us.

Faith sees into another world, another dimension. People of faith see and hear things others don't. Real faith is not fixated on the things of this world. Material prosperity does not top its list. While all the false prophets in Israel were prospering under the wicked Queen

Jezebel's favor, there were others who separated themselves and chose hardship over compromise. Chief among this group was Elijah. While the false prophets were feasting at Jezebel's table, hearing and seeing nothing, Elijah was communing with God in a small room at a widow's house where he was supernaturally sustained by God. The nation went after the big shot false prophets who hung out with the queen. Everybody was mad at Elijah. Nobody wanted to hang out with him – nobody except God. Take your pick: prosperity and compromise in the palace or communion with the living God at the widow's house?

When faith hears or sees something in

the Spirit, it goes to work to bring it about in the natural realm. Elijah demonstrates this on Mt. Carmel in 1 Kings 18. At God's word, Elijah had shut the heavens and turned off the water for over three years. There was great famine in the land. In 1 Kings 18 the word of the Lord came to him again and told him it was time to turn the water back on. When he confronted the wicked king Ahab, he told him to get all the false prophets who feasted with the evil queen Jezebel up to Mt. Carmel. His victorious faith moved him to challenge all eight-hundred-fifty of them to a showdown. He boldly declared that the true God would answer by fire. After several hours, the false prophets had been unsuccessful in their attempts to get their god to send fire and consume the sacrifice. When he called on his God, fire came out of heaven and consumed the sacrifice. The people repented and proclaimed that the God of Elijah was the true God. It had been a victorious day but there was still more to do.

Without wasting any time, Elijah ordered that all the false prophets be killed. When that was carried out Elijah heard something that nobody else heard: "And Elijah said unto Ahab, get thee up, eat and drink; for there is a sound of abundance of rain" (1 Kings 18:41). Faith hears things others don't hear. Elijah heard the sound before he saw the storm. He heard it by faith before there was a cloud in the sky. By faith he announced that a storm was coming and told Ahab to get to the palace. We next find Elijah on top of Mt. Carmel in a spiritual birthing position, travailing to bring the rain. "So, Ahab went off to eat and drink, but Elijah climbed to the top of Carmel, bent down to the ground, and put his face between his knees: (1 Kings 18:42). Faith works with God to bring things to birth in the Spirit.

Next Elijah begins looking for evidence to support what he has heard. "Go and look toward the sea," he told his servant. And he went up and looked. "There is nothing there," he said. Seven times Elijah said, "Go back." The seventh time the servant reported, "A cloud as small as a man's hand is rising from the sea." So, Elijah said, "Go and tell Ahab, 'Hitch up your chariot and go down before the rain stops you." Meanwhile, the sky grew black with clouds, the wind rose, a heavy rain started falling and Ahab rode off to Jezreel (1 Kings 18:43-45).

I am certain that Elijah had to battle discouragement when his servant returned over and over again to report that he had seen nothing. This is a picture of Elijah sending his faith out to look for the manifestation of what he had heard. Notice that he didn't give up after one or two attempts. He had persistent faith that refused to quit. Most of us would not have been too excited about the results his servant reported on his seventh trip. The sky was clear, except for one tiny cloud the size of a man's hand (v. 44). But Elijah not only heard things others didn't; by faith, he saw things others didn't. He saw the potential for a small thing. His faith took hold of that tiny cloud, and it became thunder clouds filled with rain. I wonder how many times we have failed to see the full manifestation of a miracle because we didn't recognize the potential in a small thing?

3

FAITH TO COME OUT OF THE CAVE

It takes real faith to come out of the cave. It is perplexing to see the great prophet Elijah running in fear after winning an incredible victory on Mt. Carmel (1 Kings 18). He had called fire down from heaven, led the nation to repentance, executed eight-hundred-fifty false prophets, and brought rain after a long drought. The wicked Queen Jezebel was so upset when it was reported to her that Elijah had presided over the execution of her false prophets, she sent a messenger to tell him she was going to kill him. You would think that after such a great victory with so many miracles, Elijah would have held his ground. He didn't; he ran in fear and eventually ended up hiding in a cave.

We find him next in Beersheba, so fearful and exhausted he wants to die. "Elijah was afraid and ran for his life. When he came to Beersheba in Judah, he left his servant there, while he himself went a day's journey into the wilderness. He came to a broom bush, sat down under it, and prayed that he might die. "I have had enough, LORD," he said. "Take my life; I am no better than my ancestors." Then he lay down under the bush and fell asleep" (1 Kings 19:3-5).

It is a mystery how someone can be plunged into despair so quickly after a great victory, but it is not uncommon. Take note of what Elijah is saying. It is certainly not faith talking: "I have had enough. I want to die." Have you ever heard a preacher say something like. "God only responds to faith?" There seems to be no faith in what Elijah says – just discouragement and depression. After asking God to let him die, he goes to sleep. When he wakes up an angel is there preparing him some food. He eats the cake prepared by the angel but there is still no evidence of faith in operation. He just goes back to sleep after eating. When he awakens the second time, he finds the angel cooking again. Does God only respond to faith? These encounters indicate that God in His mercy comes to help his servants in times of deep discouragement – even if they are not speaking faith.

What Elijah does next is shocking. He journeys forty days in the strength of those meals prepared by an angel. But he travels straight to a cave. It appears that he was still fearful and depressed. When God came looking for his discouraged servant he asked, "What are you doing here, Elijah?" The prophet's response indicates how deeply depressed he was: "And he said, I have been very jealous for the LORD God of hosts: for the children of Israel have forsaken thy covenant, thrown down thine altars, and slain thy prophets with the sword; and I, even I only, am left; and they seek my life, to take it away (1 Kings 19:9-10, KJV).

It is clear that Elijah's perception and thought had been disturbed by his fear and depression. But once again God demonstrates His mercy. He has no rebuke for His tired servant. He just lets him know that He has more for him to do: "And the LORD said unto him, Go, return on thy way to the wilderness of Damascus: and when thou comest, anoint

Hazael to be king over Syria: And Jehu the son of Nimshi shalt thou anoint to be king over Israel: and Elisha the son of Shaphat of Abelmeholah shalt thou anoint to be prophet in thy room. And it shall come to pass, that him that escapeth the sword of Hazael shall Jehu slay: and him that escapeth from the sword of Jehu shall Elisha slay. Yet I have left me seven thousand in Israel, all the knees which have not bowed unto Baal, and every mouth which hath not kissed him. So he departed thence, and found Elisha the son of Shaphat,.." (1 Kings 19:15-19, KJV).

God didn't forsake His servant when he was struggling. He went looking for him. When

He found him hiding in a cave, He didn't rebuke him for his fear and unbelief. He spoke gently to him and let him know that he still had more for him to do. Elijah felt like it was all over. Memories of recent victories didn't lift him out of his despair. His depression was so deep that he had asked God to let him die. But to his credit, when he heard the voice of God, he came out of the cave. God's word gave him new hope and he realized it wasn't over for him. God still had work for him to do. He rose out of his depression and went forth to obey the word of the Lord. That is real faith: obeying God's word even when you don't feel like it – even when you are depressed, fearful and hurting. Talk is cheap. Elijah could have come out of the cave talking faith; but the proof of his faith was not in his words but his actions.

Elijah thought God was through with him; maybe he even thought He was disappointed with him. Nothing was further from the truth. Sometimes our perceptions are wrong. God doesn't prepare us for years just to leave us discouraged in some cave. He comes looking for us just as He did for Elijah. However, He won't force us to come out. He will speak to us, but we must make the decision to respond to His word and come out or to remain in the cave and sink into deeper despondency. Consider what God did with

Elijah after he had given up on himself. He anointed Jehu and Hazael to be kings and he anointed Elisha to be prophet in his place. He didn't die but was carried up into heaven in a chariot. Could he have missed all this if he had refused to respond to God's word in faith and come out of the cave?

It is absolutely amazing how much God did through Elijah after he had given up on himself – and He is still not finished. The chariot ride into heaven is not the last that we hear or see of Elijah. Malachi 4:5 says, "See, I will send the prophet Elijah to you before that great and dreadful day of the LORD comes..." Jesus, when speaking of John the Baptist, said,

"Truly I tell you, among those born of women there has not risen anyone greater than John the Baptist; yet whoever is least in the kingdom of heaven is greater than he. From the days of John the Baptist until now, the kingdom of heaven has been subjected to violence, and violent people have been raiding it. For all the Prophets and the Law prophesied until John. And if you are willing to accept it, he is Elijah who was to come. Whoever has ears, let them hear. "(Matthew 11:11-14).

Elijah shows up again with Moses on the Mount of Transfiguration: "After six days Jesus took with him Peter, James, and John the brother of James, and led them up a high mountain by themselves. There he was transfigured before them. His face shone like the sun, and his clothes became as white as the light. Just then there appeared before them Moses and Elijah, talking with Jesus (Matthew 17:1-3). Some theologians believe that the two witnesses of Revelation will be Moses and Elijah (Revelation 11). Isn't it amazing to see all that God can do with someone who had been ready to give up on himself and check out?

Are you in a cave today? Are you overwhelmed by negative circumstances? Do you feel like it is all over for you? Don't believe it. Elijah felt the same way. It is too soon to quit. God may have much more for you to do.

He has not forsaken you; it is lonely in the cave, but you are not alone. God sent angels to minister to Elijah when his faith was not even functioning. He can do the same for you. Keep seeking Him and listening for His voice. When you hear Him speak, get up and get out. Your journey may be longer and more exciting than you could ever imagine in the cave. We read about Elijah because he had faith to come out of the cave. God didn't create you to be a cave dweller. Don't sit down in the darkness of fear and depression. There are valleys to cross and mountains to climb. Victory is your destiny; real faith will take you there.

4

FAITH THAT DOESN'T FAINT

When King Jehosophat was surrounded by enemies, he was overwhelmed; he didn't know what to do (2 Chronicles 20). You may feel the same way. The pressure on God's people has never been stronger. Many feel helpless and hopeless before a continual onslaught of problems. Enemy armies are everywhere, and we are greatly outnumbered. Just dealing with problems and daily responsibilities leaves us exhausted. We sometimes feel that Daniel's prophecy about worn out saints is being fulfilled in our day. When he spoke of anti-Christ in Daniel 7:25, he must have had our days in mind; many of God's people are so worn out that they have little energy left to fight spiritual enemies. "And he shall speak great words against the most High, and shall wear out the saints of the most High,…" We must receive strength from the Holy spirit to stand and fight as we approach the end of the age. When we come to the end of our strength, His is available. God promises to help and strengthen His servants: "So do not fear, for I am with you; do not be dismayed, for I am your God. I will strengthen you and help you; I will uphold you with my righteous right hand" (Isaiah 41:10).

The Bible is filled with promises to encourage us when we are surrounded by enemies or negative circumstances that cause us to feel overwhelmed. Here are just a few:

Zerrubabel was charged with rebuilding the temple that had been destroyed. He was discouraged because little progress had been made and he lacked both resources and laborers. Day after day he stared at a huge mountain of stones that were supposed to become a temple, but nothing was happening. He was feeling overwhelmed one day when the prophet Zechariah stopped by and spoke these words: "So he said to me, "This is the word of the LORD to Zerubbabel: "Not by might nor by power, but by my Spirit,' says the LORD Almighty" (Zechariah 4:6). God wanted him to know that when he was at the end of all human strength and ability, he still had reason to hope. What he could not do in his own strength, God would help him do in the power of the Spirit. Zechariah went on to encourage Zerubbabel by telling him that he had started the project and that with God's help he would be the one to finish it.

David was often taxed beyond measure. The Psalms are filled with agonizing cries for help and deliverance. Time and time again, he felt like it was all over, but faith kept him looking up and moving forward. King Saul became jealous over David's growing popularity after he conquered Goliath and attempted to kill him several times. Samuel had anointed him king, but he had to flee like a fugitive. For ten long years his life was on the line every day. He hid in caves and in the wilderness as Saul's soldiers hunted for him. All the while, he was engaging the enemies of Israel in combat. I Samuel 30 records the account of him returning to Ziklag after raiding enemy camps to find the city destroyed and all the women and children carried away captive. Samuel wrote that David and his men wept until they had no more strength to weep. At his lowest moment, his discouraged men talked of stoning him because they blamed him for the disaster. It was overwhelming but the Bible says that David encouraged himself in the Lord. God gave him direction and he pursued his enemies and recovered everything plus spoil they had taken from others. David constantly rose up out of discouragement and went forward by faith.

One of my favorite chapters in the Bible is Psalm 27. David was in constant peril from his enemies. Saul was pursuing him with the intention of killing him. He had to continually move from one hideout to another. A man with lesser faith would have never survived. David was traumatized beyond measure over and over again. No one would have blamed him for throwing his hands up in despair and giving up, but he kept going on by faith. There were times when he had to wonder why, if God had chosen him to be king, he had to live in continual danger and face unbearable pressure. But God's ways are not our ways and David knew in the depth of his being that God was using all the danger and hardship to prepare him to rule. At the end of Psalm 27, David penned these words: "I had fainted, unless I had believed to see the goodness of the LORD in the land of the living. Wait on the LORD: be of good courage, and he shall strengthen thine heart: wait, I say, on the Lord" (Psalm 27:13-14, KJV). "I had fainted" could be translated "I would have given up" or, "I would have thrown in the towel." Faith kept him going and believing for a better day. It will keep you going, too.

I mentioned King Jehosophat at the beginning of this chapter. He was surrounded by a vast enemy army. Judah was hopelessly outnumbered, but King Jehosophat had no intention of surrendering. He called the entire nation to come together to fast and pray. He closed a public prayer by saying, "We do not know what to do, but our eyes are on you" (2 Chronicles 20:12). In response to that prayer the Lord moved on a prophet named Jahaziel and he gave the following word: "Listen, King Jehoshaphat and all who live in Judah and Jerusalem! This is what the LORD says to you: "Do not be afraid or discouraged because of this vast army. For the battle is not yours, but God's" (2 Chronicles 20:15-17). He went on to give specific instructions about how to go out against the enemy. "You will not have to fight this battle. Take up your positions; stand firm and see the deliverance the LORD will give you, Judah and Jerusalem. Do not be afraid; do not be discouraged. Go out to face them tomorrow, and the LORD will be with you." Two things were required to bring the promised victory to pass: faith and action. "Have faith in the LORD your God and you will be upheld; have faith in his prophets and you will be successful (2 Chronicles 20:20)."

When the army of Judah marched out, the singers and those who played instruments were in front. The Bible says that when they began to praise the Lord, He set ambushes against the enemy. When their praise went up, God's power came down. "As they began to sing and praise, the LORD set ambushes against the men of Ammon and Moab and Mount Seir who were invading Judah, and they were defeated. The Ammonites and Moabites rose up against the men from Mount Seir to destroy and annihilate them. After they finished slaughtering the men from Seir, they helped to destroy one another" (2 Chronicles 20:22-23).

Just as God had spoken through His prophet, the army of Judah did not have to fight in the battle. After the enemies destroyed each other, Jehosophat and the army of Judah took the spoils: "So Jehoshaphat and his men went to carry off their plunder, and they found among them a great amount of equipment and clothing and also articles of value—more than they could take away. There was so much plunder that it took three days to collect it" (2 Chronicles 20:25).

Honest faith that expressed itself in the simple prayer, "We don't know what to do, but our eyes are on you," resulted in a great miracle. God heard the cry of His children and responded in power with help from above. He wants to do the same for us. Life is hard for many of God's children in these trying times. We are beset with difficulties and surrounded by spiritual enemies bent on our destruction. Fear and discouragement try to undo us, but we must not give in. We are not alone in the fight. Jesus is with us, and we have heavenly allies. Angels helped Jehosophat and the people of Judah and they will help us. If we call on Him in faith, God will ambush our enemies. He will not leave us alone in the fight. He will send help from above. "The angel of the LORD encamps around those who fear him, and he delivers them" (Psalm 34:7).

FAITH IS THE VICTORY

5

DESPERATE FAITH

Another amazing story of God's deliverance is recorded in 2 Kings 7. In this story, there is no mention of prayer being offered as it was when King Jehosophat called the entire nation to prayer in 2 Chronicles 20. Israel and Samaria were in the midst of great famine and economic distress after a long siege by the Syrian army. There must have been prayer going up as desperate people cried out to God for deliverance, but there is no evidence of faith in operation. The prophet Elisha declared that things were going to change abruptly but the king couldn't believe it. The despair among the starving multitudes was so great it is possible that everyone had given up. They waited in fear behind the walls of the city day after day expecting that at any moment the enemy would destroy them. Fear paralyzed the entire nation as the darkness of impending doom settled like a thick blanket over them. The anxiety and stress were unbearable. All hope of deliverance was gone. But God had mercy and intervened in spite of their apparent lack of faith.

Deliverance came as a result of the action of four starving lepers who were awaiting death outside the gates of the city. Their incredible story is recorded in 2 Kings 7:3-8.

"Now there were four men with leprosy at the entrance of the city gate. They said to each other, "Why stay here until we die? If we say, 'We'll go into the city'—the famine is there, and we will die. And if we stay here, we will die. So, let's go over to the camp of the Arameans (Syrians) and surrender. If they spare us, we live; if they kill us, then we die."

"At dusk they got up and went to the camp of the Arameans. When they reached the edge of the camp, no one was there, for the Lord had caused the Arameans to hear the sound of chariots and horses and a great army, so that they said to one another, "Look, the king of Israel has hired the Hittite and Egyptian kings to attack us!" So, they got up and fled in the dusk and abandoned their tents and their horses and donkeys. They left the camp as it was and ran for their lives."

Lepers were unlikely deliverers. Their bodies were literally devoured by the disease and when they went out in public they were required to cry, "Unclean! Unclean." No one would dream that God would use lepers to bring about a great deliverance – no one except those who remember that God has said, "The lame take the prey" (Isaiah 33:23, KJV). That is exactly what happened here. Four lepers got up in their hopelessness and desperation and limped toward the camp of the enemy. God made their footsteps sounds like the noise of a huge army and fear struck the hearts of the Syrian soldiers. When the lepers arrived, they discovered that the army had fled in such terror they left everything behind. They found not only food and water but gold, silver and all manner of goods. After hiding some of the spoil, they returned to the city to tell their starving countrymen about the great miracle.

Consider how this great miracle of deliverance came about. God used four starving lepers to deliver the whole nation. As they sat outside the city gate awaiting doom, God began to put thoughts in their minds. They reasoned, "If we sit here, we will die. If we go into the city, we will die. If we go to the camp of the enemy, we may die but it is possible they will spare us." They decided to get up and start walking. The only evidence of even a shred of faith is in their statement, "If they spare us, we will live." At best, it was a feeble, desperate faith – really more hope than faith. It is not the stuff that you would expect great deliverance or great victory to come out of. But God's ways are not our ways and the action of four starving lepers wrought deliverance for the whole nation.

There may be lessons for us to learn here. Let's consider, point by point, what the lepers did. We find them depressed, fearful and in great despair outside the city gate. We can only surmise why they were sitting in the dust outside the gate. It was more than likely because the abuse and rejection inside the city was more than they could bear. They were in a deplorable condition and had no idea that God was going to use them in such a mighty way. The first thing they did was weigh their options. Only one made sense so they got up and started walking. You may have heard the statement, "If you are going through hell, keep walking." That is the only sensible thing to do. If we give up and sit down in despair, we will die. The lepers made the only reasonable decision. They got up and walked out of the hell that was holding the entire nation. That decision by four broken, defeated lepers led to deliverance.

You may be going through the darkest, most difficult period of your life. These are trying times. God's people are facing pressures greater than anything they have ever experienced. Fear and anxiety constantly attack us, as they do everyone else in these troubling times of economic uncertainty and mounting pressure. The devil knows his days are numbered and he is relentless in his attacks on God's servants. The hordes of hell have been unleashed to try to discourage and defeat us. Sometimes, in the face of overwhelming struggles, we wonder if our prayers are doing any good. We question whether God is even hearing us. Our circumstances get worse and worse, and we feel powerless to change them.

We are desperate to hear God speak to us. When, after long seasons of prayer, he seems to be silent we grow more and more discouraged. Like King Jehosophat we have to say, "we don't know what to do." But we must not stop there; we must finish his prayer: "but our eyes are on you." In our worst moments, we must continue to look to Jesus. He has promised to never leave nor forsake us. He has promised to help us." (Hebrews 13:5-6). We are not alone. That is the difference between believers and those who do not know the Lord; we face many of the same problems they do but we never have to face a problem alone. Satan wants to make us feel like we are alone, like God has forsaken us, but we know that is a lie. Even if we feel like it is true, we must reject our feelings and continue reaching out to Jesus in faith. We must not doubt in the darkness what God has spoken to our hearts in the light. We must determine not to live by what we feel but by what we know; and by faith we know that God's word is true.

Next, we must begin to confess what we know to be true. When we are in desperation it is even more important for us to speak God's word in faith. We must search for promises that speak to our situation and begin to confess them out loud. It is good for your troubled mind to hear your own voice speaking God's word in faith. If you are going through hell, keep walking; and keep speaking God's word out loud in faith every step of the way. Are you discouraged? Say, "God is with me. He will help me. I will not fear" (Hebrews 13:5-6). Have you been in a struggle for a long time? Remember what Paul said in Galatians 6:9, "And let us not grow weary while doing good, for in due season we shall reap if we do not lose heart" (NKJV). Are you struggling with anxiety and fear? Read or quote Psalm 34:4, 7: "I sought the LORD, and he answered me; he delivered me from all my fears…" The angel of the LORD encamps around those who fear him, and he delivers them."

Sometimes we become desperate because we feel like we have created the mess we are in. Satan is a master at convincing us that our own mistakes have brought suffering on us and on those we love. He bombards us with accusing thoughts in order to get us to condemn ourselves. We must remember that, even if the mess is of our own making, God is merciful. After honestly facing our own mistakes and repenting, we must accept His forgiveness and move forward with faith and hope for better days. Living with continual thoughts of guilt and condemning ourselves for mistakes of the past will hinder recovery. Our only hope lies in letting go of the past and moving on in faith. We must not pull yesterday's cloud over today's sunshine or tomorrow's possibilities.

We may be in the midst of great difficulties because our faith is being tried, because Satan is attacking us, or because of the inevitable consequences of our own sin. Whatever the reason, we must believe that God is for us and that He wants to help us. He doesn't withhold help because we have sinned. If we repent, He forgives us and comes to help us recover. Knowing why we are in a struggle is not as important as knowing that whatever the reason, God is committed to help us if we trust Him. "The salvation of the righteous comes from the LORD; he is their stronghold in time of trouble. The LORD helps them and delivers them; he delivers them from the wicked and saves them, because they take refuge in him" (Psalm 37:39-40)."

We are pilgrims on the earth. We are on our way to a better place. The hope of heaven must be kept alive in our hearts. When we are in desperate places, we must not despair. We must lift up our eyes and look unto Jesus. The writer of Hebrews understood that we would pass through discouraging times on our journey toward heaven. Here is his advice in Hebrews 12:1-3: "Therefore, since we are surrounded by such a great cloud of witnesses, let us throw off everything that hinders and the sin that so easily entangles. And let us run with perseverance the race marked out for us, fixing our eyes on Jesus, the pioneer and perfecter of faith. For the joy set before him he endured the cross, scorning its shame, and sat down at the right hand of the throne of God. Consider him who endured such opposition from sinners, so that you will not grow weary and lose heart."

Has your faith become desperate because you have come to the end of yourself? Did you fail to acknowledge the Lord in all your ways? Sometimes we lean to our own understanding and pursue our own plans without fully realizing that we are not in the will of the Lord. He lets us go until we wake up but that is usually when we are in trouble. It is crucial for us to believe that, even when we have gone our own way in the strength of self will, he doesn't forsake us or leave us alone in our trouble. Our God is merciful and kind. Throughout Psalms David cries out to the Lord in his trouble – trouble that was often of his own making. Even after his great sin with Bathsheba, which brought horrible trouble and grief to his family, David had confidence that God would help him when he cried out in his brokenness.

Psalm 40 is a good example of David crying out for help in his desperation. "I waited patiently for the LORD; and He inclined to me and heard my cry. He also brought me up out of a horrible pit, out of the miry clay, and set my feet upon a rock, and established my steps" (v. 1-2, NKJV). A little farther in the Psalm he is crying out again, "Do not withhold Your tender mercies from me, O LORD; Let Your lovingkindness and Your truth continually preserve me.

For innumerable evils have surrounded me; My iniquities have overtaken me, so that I am not able to look up; They are more than the hairs of my head; Therefore my heart fails me. Be pleased, O LORD, to deliver me; O LORD, make haste to help me" (v. 11-13, NKJV)!

David had confidence to call on the Lord with desperate faith, even when he was overwhelmed by troubles that had resulted from his own sin, because he knew that the Lord was full of loving kindness and tender mercy. "Bless the LORD, O my soul; And all that is within me, *bless* His holy name! Bless the LORD, O my soul, And forget not all His benefits: Who forgives all your iniquities, Who heals all your diseases, Who redeems your life from destruction, Who crowns you with lovingkindness and tender mercies..." (Psalm 103:1-4, NKJV).

A beautiful picture of God's mercy to those who are in trouble because of their sin is found in the book of Hosea. God instructed Hosea to take a wife from among the prostitutes. His family and friends must have wondered if he had lost his mind, but God had a purpose in it. He knew she would be unfaithful to him, yet Hosea would go seek her and take her back into his home. This was to be a prophetic picture of God's relationship with unfaithful Israel. "When the LORD began to speak through Hosea, the LORD said to him, "Go, marry a promiscuous woman and have children with her, for like an adulterous wife this land is guilty of unfaithfulness to the LORD." So, he married Gomer daughter of Diblaim..." (Hosea 1:2-3).

Gomer was unfaithful as expected and great difficulty came upon her because of her sin. In spite of her unfaithfulness, Hosea loved her and forgave her just as God loved and forgave backsliding Israel when she repented.

After turning from the Lord and following her own desires, Gomer (Israel) found herself filled with despair, in bitter circumstances. God allowed her to continue on her sinful path until she was broken and utterly hopeless. He had every right to cast her away, but His mercy wouldn't allow it. Because of His great love, he went searching for her and when He found her, He forgave her and redeemed her life from destruction. "Therefore, I am now going to allure her; I will lead her into the wilderness and speak tenderly to her. There I will give her back her vineyards and will make the Valley of Achor a door of hope. There she will respond as in the days of her youth, as in the day she came up out of Egypt" (Hosea 2:14-15).

When we are discouraged because of the oppression of the enemy or the consequences of our sin, Satan wants to make us think that God is a harsh judge. He wants us to live in fear and despair of forgiveness. He tries to paint a picture in our minds of God as a merciless judge and prevent us from seeing Him as a loving Father. We need to reject the images Satan impresses on our minds and replace them with images from the Bible. It is imperative that we remember how he treated David after his terrible sins of adultery and murder. When David repented, He forgave him and later said that David was a man after his own heart. When Gomer returned to her unfaithfulness and adultery, He searched for her, even allured her, and extended mercy to her. The Bible is filled with accounts of God's great mercy and love.

When Gomer came to her senses, she was in the Valley Of Achor, which means bitterness. Sin had robbed her of joy and made everything bitter in her life. She realized her mistake, but she felt helpless and abandoned. She probably thought within herself, "Who would want me now?" But God didn't leave her alone to find her way back to Him; He went searching for her. He allured her. Allure has the meaning of attracting with something desirable. What is more desirable to a guilty sinner than the hope of mercy, forgiveness, and restoration? God said that he was going to give vineyards back to her (Remember that Gomer symbolizes the nation of Israel). He was going to restore what she had lost because of her sin and self-will.

This is amazing love. The woman who had forsaken her husband for other lovers, the nation which had forsaken her God, was being restored by the One who had been wronged. It is the business of the devil to destroy us; God is always looking for an opportunity to deliver and restore us. Hosea 2:15 offers hope in the place of bitterness. God said that He would make the Valley of Achor (bitterness) a door of hope. This is amazing love! God doesn't simply offer hope; He transforms the place of bitterness into a doorway of hope. Gomer, nor Israel, has to spend the rest of her days in shame and bitterness. God offers hope that will enable her to walk away from the sin and shame and walk into a future filled with hope and mercy. If you feel like you are going through hell on earth, keep walking. Don't sit down in your bitterness and despair. You are not condemned to live the rest of your days in the Valley of Achor. Your loving Father is going to swing wide the door of hope and lead you out of despair into joy and peace in His presence.

We must have great faith in God's mercy. Without it the devil will continually beat us to death with guilt, shame, and condemnation. We must believe that God will respond to desperate faith that wants to return to the Father's house. The story of the Prodigal Son in Luke 15 is a great picture of God's love and mercy. The youngest son of a wealthy man asked for his inheritance and squandered it on parties and wild living. When the money was gone his "friends" deserted him and he began living a nightmare. Condemned by his own sin, too ashamed to even lift his head, he couldn't bear the thought of humbling himself to return to the father's house. But after a season of feeding pigs and eating their food, he came to his senses. That is what God wants. It grieves Him to see us suffering, whether it is because of our own sin or because of tribulation in this life, but His hope is that the suffering will cause us to reach out to Him in our time of need. Nothing illustrates this better than the return of the prodigal to the father's house.

"When he came to his senses, he said, 'How many of my father's hired servants have food to spare, and here I am starving to death! I will set out and go back to my father and say to him: Father, I have sinned against heaven and against you. I am no longer worthy to be called your son; make me like one of your hired servants.' So, he got up and went to his father.

"But while he was still a long way off, his father saw him and was filled with compassion for him; he ran to his son, threw his arms around him, and kissed him.

"The son said to him, 'Father, I have sinned against heaven and against you. I am no longer worthy to be called your son.'

"But the father said to his servants, 'Quick! Bring the best robe and put it on him. Put a ring on his finger and sandals on his feet. Bring the fattened calf and kill it. Let's have a feast and celebrate. For this son of mine was dead and is alive again; he was lost and is found.' So, they began to celebrate" (Luke 15:17-24).

The prodigal didn't know the depth of his father's love. He was expecting condemnation for his foolishness, not celebration for his return. He was ready to live as a servant in his father's house but that thought had never entered his father's mind. The son was probably planning to fall at his father's feet and beg for mercy, but he never had the chance. His father couldn't contain his joy when he saw him coming up the road. He didn't wait for him to walk up and knock on the door. He ran out to meet him, embraced him, and immediately began making plans for a great celebration. Everyone in the household was happy except the prodigal's self-righteous older brother.

If you are in trouble because of negative circumstances, you need not live in condemnation, even if your own mistakes or sin have created the mess. Your heavenly Father is more merciful than the prodigal's earthly father. A prayer as simple as, "I don't know what to do, but my eyes are on You," will bring Him running down the road. He has been waiting for you to come to your senses. He meant it when He said, "I will help you." Keep walking; keep looking up. Don't despise desperate faith; it always gets God's attention. Your valley of bitterness may soon become a door of hope. You are not condemned to live the rest of your life defeated and struggling because you have failed or fallen down. Real faith – even if it is desperate – will bring you to victory. "This is the victory that has overcome the world, even our faith" (1 John 5:4).

6

FAITH TO SLAY A GIANT

Faith that slays giants is faith that magnifies the Lord; it looks at God instead of the problem. Magnify God and the problem seems smaller. Magnify the problem and God seems smaller. It will make you feel smaller, too. That's what giants do. They make you feel small and inadequate by intimidating you. It takes strong faith – real faith that focuses on God, not the problem – to overcome them. The people of God in the Old Testament battled physical giants; we battle spiritual ones.

The children of Israel were intimidated by reports of giants in the Promised Land. Twelve spies were sent to explore the land. Ten brought back a negative report. All they could talk about was how big the giants were. Two, Joshua and Caleb, brought back a positive report; they talked about how big the grapes were. Unfortunately, the majority prevailed. The negative report of the ten spies resulted in fear and intimidation. The entire first generation failed to cross the Jordan River. They turned back to the wilderness and perished in their unbelief. Only Joshua and Caleb survived to enter Canaan with the next generation. Faith made the difference. Joshua and Caleb had the kind of faith that focused on God and magnified Him instead of the problem.

Numbers 13 records the account of the spies. The results of focusing on the obstacles instead of looking to God in faith are easily seen. "There they reported to them and to the whole assembly and showed them the fruit of the land. They gave Moses this account: "We went into the land to which you sent us, and it does flow with milk and honey! Here is its fruit. But the people who live there are powerful, and the cities are fortified and very large. We even saw descendants of Anak there (Numbers

13:26-28). The descendants of Anak were giants.

The difference in perspective is revealed as the report continues; one is the perspective of unbelief, the other of victorious faith. "Then Caleb silenced the people before Moses and said, "We should go up and take possession of the land, for we can certainly do it."

But the men who had gone up with him said, "We can't attack those people; they are stronger than we are." And they spread among the Israelites a bad report about the land they had explored. They said, "The land we explored devours those living in it. All the people we saw there are of great size. We saw the Nephilim there (the descendants of Anak come from the Nephilim). We seemed like grasshoppers in our own eyes, and we looked the same to them" (Numbers 13:30-33).

Joshua and Caleb said, "We can." The other ten spies said, "We can't." It is evident that they were looking at the obstacles. Looking through eyes of faith gives us a different outlook or perspective. It causes us to focus more on possibilities than on problems. The language of the ten spies reveals the depth of the unbelief which completely clouded their perspective. The way they viewed the giants affected the way they viewed themselves. Their words conditioned them for defeat and failure. There was no point in them attempting to fight the giants. Their attitude would have defeated them before they ever entered the battle. Grasshoppers don't slay giants.

Faith produces courage and strength. Faith enabled Joshua and Caleb to believe the Word of God. He had promised to give them the land. In their minds, the size of the inhabitants made no difference. Faith in the promise of God was greater than fear of the giants. Caleb's faith to cross over the Jordan River and launch the attack seems even stronger in the language of the New King James Version: "Let us go up at once and take possession, for we are well able to overcome it" (Numbers 13:30).

The struggle between faith and unbelief continues into Numbers 14. The power of unbelief to produce fear and negative perception and attitude is shocking. The influence of the negative report of the ten spies is almost unbelievable. People who had seen years of daily miracles were reduced to crying, pity and paralyzing fear by one negative report. Their faith was destroyed and all hope of possessing the land was surrendered. They had no regard for the promise of God. They were ready to retreat and return to slavery in Egypt.

"So, all the congregation lifted up their voices and cried, and the people wept that night. And all the children of Israel complained against Moses and Aaron, and the whole congregation said to them, "If only we had died in the land of Egypt! Or if only we had died in this wilderness! Why has the LORD brought us to this land to fall by the sword, that our wives and children should become victims? Would it not be better for us to return to Egypt?" So, they said to one another, "Let us select a leader and return to Egypt" (Numbers 14:1-4).

Joshua and Caleb had a completely different opinion. They were so upset over what they were hearing that they tore their clothes and pleaded with the people to reconsider. The fearful spies were afraid that they would be devoured by the giants and their fear affected nearly the whole multitude. Joshua and Caleb viewed the giants as food for their faith. They saw themselves as the devourers and not the devoured. "…they are bread for us" (v.9, KJV).

"But Joshua the son of Nun and Caleb the son of Jephunneh, *who were* among those who had spied out the land, tore their clothes; and they spoke to all the congregation of the children of Israel, saying: "The land we passed through to spy out *is* an exceedingly good land. If the LORD delights in us, then He will bring us into this land and give it to us, 'a land which flows with milk and honey.' Only do not rebel against the LORD, nor fear the people of the land, for they *are* our bread; their protection has departed from them, and the LORD *is* with us. Do not fear them" (Numbers 14:6-9, NKJV).

The faith of Joshua and Caleb lasted a long time. It endured thirty-eight more years in the wilderness. It outlived all the unbelievers of the first generation who were afraid of the giants. It brought them back to the Promised Land to lead the charge with the new generation. It sent them without hesitation across the flooding Jordan River. It gave them courage to march on Jericho, the most strongly fortified city in the land. The giants hadn't grown in thirty-eight years, but they had probably multiplied. That was no concern to Joshua and Caleb. Their faith had grown stronger with waiting. They did not hesitate to obey the word of the Lord and go forward to possess the land.

Joshua knew that his faith was up to the challenge, but he was taking no chances. He carefully selected only two spies to explore the land. They came back with a report of faith – giant slaying faith. "The LORD has surely given the whole land into our hands; all the people are melting in fear because of us" (Joshua 2:24). Not a negative word was spoken by anyone. The second generation was different than the first. No one entertained ideas of going back. The force of their faith was quickly felt by their enemies. "Now when all the Amorite kings west of the Jordan and all the Canaanite kings along the coast heard how the LORD had dried up the Jordan before the Israelites until they had crossed over, their hearts melted in fear and they no longer had the courage to face the Israelites" (Joshua 5:1).

Joshua led the army of Israel from victory to victory. After one of the most successful military campaigns in history, Caleb was ready to possess the land Moses had promised him. His courage should inspire every would be giant slayer on the planet. He was eighty-five years old when he asked for Joshua's blessing to destroy the giants who were trespassing on his mountain. "So here I am today, eighty-five years old! I am still as strong today as the day Moses sent me out; I'm just as vigorous to go out to battle now as I was then. Now give me this hill country that the LORD promised me that day. You yourself heard then that the Anakites were there, and their cities were large and fortified, but, the LORD helping me, I will drive them out just as he said."

Then Joshua blessed Caleb son of Jephunneh and gave him Hebron as his inheritance. So Hebron has belonged to Caleb son of

Jephunneh the Kenizzite ever since, because he followed the LORD, the God of Israel, wholeheartedly. (Hebron used to be called Kiriath Arba after Arba, who was the greatest man among the Anakites)" (Joshua 14:10-15).

Without question, the most famous giant slayer of all time is a young shepherd named David. We meet him on the field of battle in 1 Samuel 17. He was too young to be a soldier, but he was not too young to slay a giant. When he arrived at the battlefield with some food for his brothers, they wanted him to get back home right away. He was just a kid, and they didn't think he belonged with the army. But something came over David when he saw

Goliath and heard him defying the God of Israel and her armies. He couldn't believe that the mighty King Saul or one of the brave soldiers had not gone down to the valley to take his head off. Then he realized that the entire army was paralyzed with fear. They had been looking at the giant for too long; David kept his eyes on God.

Here are excerpts from the account in 1 Samuel 17:4-57.

"A champion named Goliath, who was from Gath, came out of the Philistine camp… and   stood and shouted to the ranks of Israel, "Why do you come out and line up for battle?

Am I not a Philistine, and are you not the servants of Saul? Choose a man and have him come down to me. If he is able to fight and kill me, we will become your subjects; but if I overcome him and kill him, you will become our subjects and serve us." Then the Philistine said, "This day I defy the armies of Israel! Give me a man and let us fight each other." On hearing the Philistine's words, Saul and all the Israelites were dismayed and terrified" (1 Samuel 17:4, 8-11).

David learned that Goliath had been defying the armies of Israel for forty days. He had challenged a man to come and fight with him over and over again but not one dared.

David had heard enough. When none of the adults volunteered to go shut the defiant giant's mouth, he volunteered for the job. "David left his things with the keeper of supplies, ran to the battle lines, and asked his brothers how they were. As he was talking with them, Goliath, the Philistine champion from Gath, stepped out from his lines and shouted his usual defiance, and David heard it. Whenever the Israelites saw the man, they all fled from him in great fear" (1 Samuel 17:22-24).

David couldn't believe it. He was even more astounded that the giant was still wearing his head when he discovered that the king had offered a great reward to the man who defeated him. "Now the Israelites had been saying, "Do you see how this man keeps coming out? He comes out to defy Israel. The king will give great wealth to the man who kills him. He will also give him his daughter in marriage and will exempt his family from taxes in Israel."

David asked the men standing near him, "What will be done for the man who kills this Philistine and removes this disgrace from Israel? Who is this uncircumcised Philistine that he should defy the armies of the living God?" They repeated to him what they had been saying and told him, "This is what will be done for the man who kills him" (1 Samuel 17:25-27).

His brothers treated him like a little kid and angrily told him to go home but by then he had Saul's attention. "What David said was overheard and reported to Saul, and Saul sent for him.

David said to Saul, "Let no one lose heart on account of this Philistine; your servant will go and fight him."

Saul replied, "You are not able to go out against this Philistine and fight him; you are only a young man, and he has been a warrior from his youth."

But David said to Saul, "Your servant has been keeping his father's sheep. When a lion or a bear came and carried off a sheep from the flock, I went after it, struck it, and rescued the sheep from its mouth. When it turned on me, I seized it by its hair, struck it and killed it. Your servant has killed both the lion and the bear; this uncircumcised Philistine will be like one of them, because he has defied the armies of the living God. The LORD who rescued me from the paw of the lion and the paw of the bear will rescue me from the hand of this Philistine."

Saul said to David, "Go, and the LORD be with you" (1Samuel 17:31-37).

Saul quickly changed his attitude toward David. At first, he viewed him as his older brothers did. The New International Version has Saul calling David a young man in verse 33. The King James Version translates it a bit differently: "You are just a youth." The implication was that David was just a kid who had no business being there, but as Saul listened, he quickly formed a different opinion of David. There is something compelling about the faith of a giant slayer. It is highly unlikely that Saul had ever encountered a teenager who had slain a lion and a bear, much less one who had slain them with his bare hands. It is almost beyond belief that an army of tough, seasoned soldiers would let a teenager go down to face a giant who was a veteran soldier – a champion of many battles. David must have demonstrated incredible faith and confidence to earn such an honor. Then again, he may have been Saul's only hope; no one else was signing up for the job and, although he was a great warrior, it didn't appeal to Saul either.

So, a teenager defied the giant that had been defying the army of Israel and its God every day for forty days. David ran toward him with confidence that the God the giant had defied would do him in. Giant slayers don't do what they do in their own strength. That would be impossible. They run to the battle because they have faith in a God who is much bigger than the giants. That is what set David apart from every soldier in the army. They were all magnifying Goliath; David magnified God. The soldiers looked at Goliath and said, "He is too big to kill." David looked at God and said, "He is too big to miss."

After refusing Saul's armor and weapons, David picked up five smooth stones, took his sling out of his belt, and approached the giant with confidence. Goliath had the same attitude toward David that everyone else held: He was just a boy. He did not try to hide his disdain for him.

"Then he took his staff in his hand, chose five smooth stones from the stream, put them in the pouch of his shepherd's bag and, with his sling in his hand, approached the Philistine.

Meanwhile, the Philistine, with his shield bearer in front of him, kept coming closer to David. He looked David over and saw that he was little more than a boy, glowing with health and handsome, and he despised him. He said to David, "Am I a dog that you come at me with sticks?" And the Philistine cursed David by his gods. "Come here," he said, "and I'll give your flesh to the birds and the wild animals" (1 Samuel 17:40-44)!

David was not impressed with Goliath's arrogant attitude and he wasted no time before he started trash talking the bewildered giant. It is easy to see that David's confidence was in the Lord. He knew that the God he worshipped didn't appreciate uncircumcised Philistines defying Him. This had become His battle. David knew he was just the delivery boy. He also knew that his faith would make him a rich hero. He gladly seized the opportunity. "David said to the Philistine, "You come against me with sword and spear and javelin, but I come against you in the name of the LORD Almighty, the God of the armies of Israel, whom you have defied. This day the LORD will deliver you into my hands, and I'll strike you down and cut off your head. This very day I will give the carcasses of the Philistine army to the birds and the wild animals, and the whole world will know that there is a God in Israel. All those gathered here will know that it is not by sword or spear that the LORD saves; for the battle is the LORD's, and he will give all of you into our hands" (1 Samuel 17:45-47).

David convinced himself of the impending victory by speaking words of faith — words that were rooted in confidence in a God who was much bigger than the giant. David did not yield to fear as Goliath came closer. He ran at his enemy and struck him before he had a chance to lift his sword. I always wonder if David was that good or if an angel zipped past and delivered the stone. However, it was delivered, it got the job done. Goliath grabbed his forehead in shock and disbelief and cried, "Nothing like this ever entered my mind before!" The victory was swift, and David wasted no time taking off his head. Courage returned to the army of Israel when the kid, the shepherd boy, held up the head of the bearded giant like a trophy. Now he could put another notch on his gun; now his resume could be updated: David – lion tamer, bear trainer, and giant slayer.

"As the Philistine moved closer to attack him, David ran quickly toward the battle line to meet him. Reaching into his bag and taking out a stone, he slung it and struck the Philistine on the forehead. The stone sank into his forehead, and he fell face down on the ground.

"So, David triumphed over the Philistine with a sling and a stone; without a sword in his hand, he struck down the Philistine and killed him. David ran and stood over him. He took hold of the Philistine's sword and drew it from the sheath. After he killed him, he cut off his head with the sword" (1 Samuel 17:48-51). David was still carrying Goliath's head when Abner took him to the palace and presented him to Saul (v. 57). The Philistines fled in terror and Israel pursued them with renewed courage. Faith is the victory.

7

FAITH IN THE BLOOD

Our victory is secured by the blood. No devil can defeat us when we stand in faith on the blood-soaked soil of Calvary. Anointing and authority are conferred on believers who by faith have appropriated the benefits of the shed blood of Jesus. Satan destroyed himself at the Cross because he failed to understand the power of sinless blood. His victory celebration was short lived because the life in sinless blood is an eternal, indestructible life. His kingdom was thrown into utter chaos when the One he thought had been destroyed invaded the regions of darkness. The Lamb of God had become the Lord of Glory and hell could not stand before him. He stripped Satan of his authority and left with the keys of hell and death.

Suddenly Satan understood what Jesus had spoken to His disciples in Matthew 16:17-19. It dawned on him that by orchestrating the Crucifixion he had sealed his fate. His kingdom would be overthrown, and mere mortals would have authority to resist and defeat him. Jesus replied, "Blessed are you, Simon son of Jonah, for this was not revealed to you by flesh and blood, but by my Father in heaven… And I tell you that you are Peter, and on this rock, I will build my church, and the gates of Hades will not overcome it. I will give you the keys of the kingdom of heaven; whatever you bind on earth will be bound in heaven, and whatever you loose on earth will be loosed in heaven."

Faith in the power of the blood assures us of victory. It enables us to triumph in the battle of the ages. In the final conflict with Satan and his hosts, faith in the blood prevails. "Then war broke out in heaven. Michael and his angels fought against the dragon, and the dragon and his angels fought back. But he was not strong enough, and they lost their place in heaven. The great dragon was hurled down—that ancient serpent called the devil, or Satan, who leads the whole world astray. He was hurled to the earth, and his angels with him.

Then I heard a loud voice in heaven say:

"Now have come the salvation and the power and the kingdom of our God, and the authority of his Messiah. For the accuser of our brothers and sisters, who accuses them before our God day and night, has been hurled down. They triumphed over him by the blood of the Lamb and by the word of their testimony; they did not love their lives so much as to shrink from death" (Revelation 12:7-11).

The Holy Spirit is poured out where the blood has been applied. Satan knew that he was in big trouble on the Day of Pentecost. Blood-bought believers climbed the stairs to the Upper Room filled with confusion and fear. They came out filled with faith and power. Peter had been afraid to admit that he was a follower of Jesus. On the day of Pentecost, he preached boldly to those who were responsible for the Crucifixion. The baptism in the Holy Spirit made the difference. The Holy Spirit was now able to do more than anoint the servants of the Lord; because of the blood, He could now indwell them. The devil was disturbed because the anointing on the emboldened believers looked and felt a lot like the anointing that had been on Jesus. The revival that began in an Upper Room in Jerusalem has filled the earth. Satan has tried everything to stop it; his efforts have all been in vain. God's Spirit is being poured out on all flesh and Satan knows he cannot contain it. "Of the increase of His government and peace, there will be no end, upon the throne of David and over His kingdom, to order it and establish it with judgment and justice, from that time forward, even forever. The zeal of the LORD of hosts will perform this" (Isaiah 9:7, NKJV).

We have witnessed the power of the Holy Spirit poured out in many nations. At an open-air crusade in Choma, Zambia, over fifty people were spontaneously filled with the Spirit. The power of witchcraft was broken, and numerous pastors testified of a release of God's power in the area which continued for years after the crusade. On the night of the spontaneous outpouring of the Spirit, many demon possessed people were delivered. A great blow was administered to the kingdom of darkness.

The breakthrough followed a confrontation with the leading witch doctor in the region. When he walked on to the crusade grounds during one of our nightly meetings, everything came to a standstill. He had ruled the area unchallenged for many years. The crowd was paralyzed with fear the moment he walked on the field. I soon understood why. He walked directly in front of the platform and our eyes were immediately fixed on one another. I felt as if liquid evil was flowing out of those eyes and sweeping over me in waves. I had battled witchcraft and witch doctors on several occasions, but I had never experienced anything like what came at me that night.

I had an eerie sensation that the platform was moving under me. For the first time in over thirty-five years of worldwide ministry, I was unable to continue preaching. I became confused and could not preach coherently. That is when I forgot my sermon and began quoting Scripture. I quoted every verse that came up out of my spirit that made reference to the power and authority of Jesus. The witch doctor was still staring intently at me when I came to Revelation 12:11, but as I quoted that verse, he vanished. He was there one moment and gone the next. "They overcame him by the blood of the Lamb and the word of their testimony." I continued to testify about the power of the blood and the frozen people came alive. A surge of faith swept through the crowd and demons began crying out. At the same moment, the Holy Spirit was poured out. The ushers and intercessors were busy for hours after the close of the meeting. Faith in the power of the blood brought a great victory. I shudder to think what might have happened had I not memorized those verses on power and authority early in my ministry.

I reminded the crowd that we must speak the Word of God in faith just as Jesus did when He defeated Satan in Matthew 4:1-11. "Then Jesus was led by the Spirit into the wilderness to be tempted by the devil. After fasting forty days and forty nights, he was hungry. The tempter came to him and said, "If you are the Son of God, tell these stones to become bread."

Jesus answered, "It is written: 'Man shall not live on bread alone, but on every word that comes from the mouth of God.'"

Then the devil took him to the holy city and had him stand on the highest point of the temple. "If you are the Son of God," he said, "throw yourself down. For it is written: "He will command his angels concerning you, and they will lift you up in their hands, so that you will not strike your foot against a stone."

Jesus answered him, "It is also written: 'Do not put the Lord your God to the test.'"

Again, the devil took him to a very high mountain and showed him all the kingdoms of the world and their splendor. "All this I will give you," he said, "if you will bow down and worship me."

Jesus said to him, "Away from me, Satan! For it is written: 'Worship the Lord your God and serve him only.' Then the devil left him, and angels came and attended him."

The power and authority in the Word of God is released when we speak it by faith. The blood-bought victory of Calvary must be enforced by faith. When Jesus shed His holy blood on the Cross, judgment was passed on Satan and the kingdom of darkness. A sentence of total destruction on him and his kingdom was pronounced. Pardon and forgiveness were conferred on believers when Jesus presented his own blood at heaven's altar. Authority was delegated to the followers of Jesus. We were given power of attorney to operate in His name: "Jesus called his twelve disciples to him and gave them authority to drive out impure spirits and to heal every disease and sickness" (Matthew 10:1). Jesus extended that authority to all believers in Mark 16:17, "And these signs will accompany those who believe: In my name they will drive out demons;…" Psalm 149 implies that believers have a part to carry out the judgment and execute the sentence pronounced against Satan and the kingdom of darkness: "Let the saints be joyful in glory; Let them sing aloud on their beds. Let the high praises of God *be* in their mouth, And a two-edged sword in their hand, To execute vengeance on the nations, And punishments on the peoples; To bind their kings with chains, And their nobles with fetters of iron; To execute on them the written judgment—This honor have all His saints" (v. 5-9, NKJV).

We would have no authority and no victory without the blood of Jesus which has cleansed us and made us righteous before God. But through the power of the blood, we have become executioners of the sentence pronounced against evil. Faith in the blood brings victory over sin, death, and the devil. Knowing this, it is disturbing that the message of the blood is little, if ever, preached in some churches today. We should be shouting it from the housetops. The Cross is central to credible Christianity and without the blood the Cross has no power or efficacy. The Resurrection followed the Crucifixion because there is power in the blood. The Resurrection validates the sacrifice of Jesus on the Cross; it proves that the resurrection life of Jesus, poured out with the blood He shed on Calvary, is eternal and indestructible. Why would any real Christian downplay, or remain silent about, the power of the blood. We are defeated without it. We are victorious by proclaiming it in faith.

The blood of Jesus is continually speaking on my behalf. I would be a fool to remain silent about it. "But you have come to…God the Judge of all, to the spirits of just men made perfect, to Jesus the Mediator of the new covenant, and to the blood of sprinkling that speaks better things than *that of* Abel" (Hebrews 12:24-25, NKJV).

What are the better things the blood of Jesus speaks? It says that we have mercy and forgiveness. It declares that we are not guilty of sin and that we are free of condemnation. It proclaims that we have been redeemed and translated from the Kingdom of Darkness to the Kingdom of Light. It affirms that we are free of condemnation and righteous in the sight of God. It announces that we are kings and priests before God with authority to rule on the earth. Why in God's name would any sincere believer be reticent to speak boldly about the precious blood of the Lamb?

The victory of faith is just empty words apart from genuine faith in the blood of Jesus. Christianity is just another religion without the blood. The shedding of sinless blood and the Resurrection are what separate Christianity from all other religions. Without the blood, and faith in its power, Christianity is as powerless to save as all the others. We should be all over the attempts of some in the Church to silence the message of the blood. Years ago, I caused quite a stir at a church growth conference. The speaker was explaining the seeker friendly philosophy of ministry when he made the following statement: "We must be careful about using theological terms like justification, redemption, and propitiation with the unchurched; it will confuse them. We must be especially cautious about talking about the blood of Jesus; it will offend them." I was shocked that no one else asked for clarification. I knew that at that very moment the blood was speaking in heaven for me; I could not remain silent. The speaker was upset, but not nearly as upset as the Spirit of God in me who seizes every opportunity to glorify Jesus and bear witness to the power of the blood.

The faulty reasoning of that speaker was shared by many others who embraced his philosophy of ministry. You can now attend churches throughout the country and never hear a sermon or sing a song about the blood of Jesus. You might as well attend a service at a Hindu or Buddhist temple. If you extract the blood from Christianity, it is no longer Christianity. Without the blood, Christianity is just one more religion without power to redeem

from sin. Just thinking about this makes me want to sing "There is a fountain filled with blood drawn from Emmanuel's veins; And sinners plunged beneath that flood lose all their guilty stains" (William Cowper, 1772). It makes me want to stand in front of churches that have embraced this watered-down philosophy of ministry and shout "There is power, power, wonder working power in the blood of the Lamb; There is power, power, wonder working power
in the precious blood of the Lamb" (Lewis E. Jones, 1899).

Why would any sincere Christian hesitate to talk about or testify of the power of the blood?

We have no standing with God apart from the blood of Jesus. It is "the blood of Jesus Christ his son 'that' cleanses us from all sin" (1 John 1:9).

Our identity, our very ground of being, depends on the blood. The victory of faith is married to our testimony of the blood of Jesus. Our hope of resurrection and eternal life depends on what we believe about the blood: "…who through the blood of the eternal covenant brought back from the dead our Lord Jesus... (Hebrews 13:20).

The victorious life of God could not dwell in us had we not been made righteous by the blood of Jesus. We have no life apart from it: "For the life of the flesh is in the blood, and I have given it to you upon the altar to make atonement for your souls; for it is the blood that makes atonement for the soul" (Leviticus 17:11, NKJV).

It is through faith in the blood of Christ that we have been redeemed: "In him we have redemption through his blood, the forgiveness of sins..." (Ephesians 1:7). "... he entered the

Most Holy Place once for all by his own blood, thus obtaining eternal redemption" (Hebrews 9:12). "For you know that it was not with perishable things such as silver or gold that you were redeemed from the empty way of life handed down to you from your ancestors, but with the precious blood of Christ, a lamb without blemish or defect" (1 Peter 1:18-19).

The blood qualified me to be translated into the kingdom: "Who hath delivered us from the power of darkness, and hath translated us into the kingdom of his dear Son: In whom we have redemption through his blood, even the forgiveness of sins" (Colossians 1:13, KJV).

It is only by the blood that we are able to enter the presence of a holy God. "But now in Christ Jesus you who once were far away have been brought near by the blood of Christ" (Ephesians 2:13). "Therefore, brethren, having boldness to enter the Holiest by the blood of Jesus, by a new and living way which He consecrated for us, through the veil, that is, His flesh, and having a High Priest over the house of God, let us draw near with a true heart in full assurance of faith, having our hearts sprinkled from an evil conscience and our bodies washed with pure water" (Hebrews 10:19-22).

The blood made it possible for Jesus to make us kings and priests with authority to rule on the earth: "…with your blood you purchased for God persons from every tribe and language and people and nation. You have made them to be a kingdom and priests to serve our God, and they will reign on the earth" (Revelation 5:9-10). "To Him who loved us and washed us from our sins in His own blood and has made us kings and priests to His God and Father, to Him be glory and dominion forever and ever. Amen" (Revelation 1:5-6, NKJV).

The list could go on and on. There is power in the blood of Jesus to save to the uttermost. How could we be silent about it? We cannot refrain from speaking about the precious blood that has saved us from our sin and delivered us from Satan's power. We are compelled to boldly proclaim the authority of that name of Jesus and plead the blood that empowers us to exercise that authority. We will confidently assault the powers of darkness and boldly declare, "Satan, the blood of Jesus is for us and against you. We have victory through faith in the blood."

Why am I here? What is my purpose?

If you're like most people, you have a lot of questions you would like to have answered: Questions like, "Who am I?" "Why am I here?" "What does the future hold?" "What's life all about anyway?"

I used to ask the same questions. I often found myself sighing, **"There's got to be more to life than this."** There was an empty, unfulfilled feeling inside of me, a lonely ache in my heart. I tried just about everything to fill up that emptiness but nothing worked.

I was depressed, lonely, confused . . . and the merry-go-round I was riding on wouldn't stop to let me off! I was ready to give up on life. After trying everything I could think of there was still something missing. My life had no meaning. The emptiness was still there.

After trying everything else I turned to God for help. I was born again when I received Jesus as my Lord and Savior. He answered my questions. He filled the emptiness in my heart. He gave me peace, love and purpose in life. And I know **He wants to do the same thing for you!**

The Bible says that *"God loved the world so much that He gave His only begotten Son so that anyone who believes in Him shall not perish but have eternal life"* (John 3:16). Jesus said of Himself, *"I am the Way - yes, and the Truth and the Life, No one can come to the Father except by Me"* (John 14:6). He said, *"I have come that **you** might have life and have it abundantly"* (John 10:10).

I'm glad you decided to read this brief message. Now, my prayer is that you will do what I did - enter into a personal relationship with God by receiving Jesus Christ as your Savior.

There would never be a better time than right now to accept God's offer of love and forgiveness . . . *"For the wages of sin is death, but the gift of God is eternal life through Jesus Christ our Lord"* (Romans 6:23).

Have you decided to accept God's offer? Here's how to do it:

Believe on the Lord Jesus (Romans 10:9)

Repent or turn from the old way of life (Luke 13:3)

Confess your sins and ask God to forgive you (1 John 1:9)

Ask Jesus to save you (Romans 10:13)

If you are really sincere, say a prayer like this one:

God, I know I'm a sinner and I need forgiveness. I ask you to forgive my sins. Jesus, I open the door of my life to you and receive you as my Savior.

Are your sins really forgiven? Did Jesus really come into your life? Here's what the Bible says: *"If we confess our sins He forgives us and cleanses us from all unrighteousness"* (1 John 1:9). *"Behold I stand at the door and knock. If anyone opens the door I will come in"* (Revelation 3:20).

This is just the beginning of a new life for you! Try to find a good church, where you can share your experience with other Christians.

Made in the USA
Middletown, DE
25 August 2024